HERBS, TREES AND TRADITIONS OF CEPHALONIA

ANNA-MARIA SIMPSON

HERBS, TREES AND TRADITIONS OF CEPHALONIA

Illustrations by
GERASIMOS RAZIS-GALIATSATOS

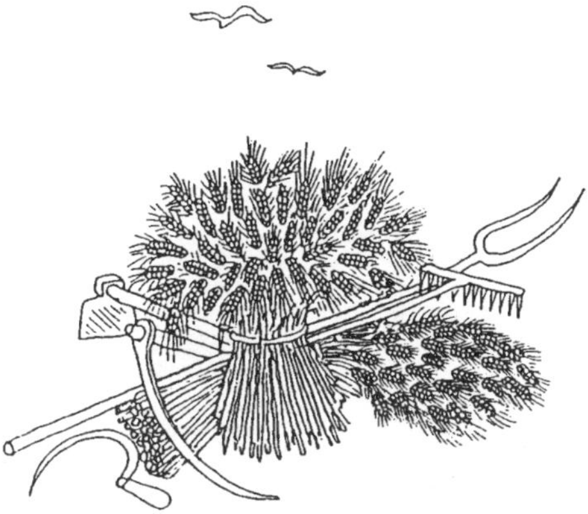

To the Earth, The Mother of All

I will sing to the Earth, the mother of all,
with steadfast foundations, most ancient, who feeds all things;
as many as traverse this sacred land and as many as inhabit the sea
and as many as fly, they are fed out of thy riches....

Hymn 30. HOMER, 8th century BC

ISBN 960-86481-0-6

Published by The Friends of Ancient Wisdom Society 1999
Distribution: 14 Ioannis Phokas, Phokata, Cephalonia 28100, Greece.

Design and cover: Anna Maria Simpson
Produced in Greece by Memigraf

Note: References to medicinal and folk use of herbs in this book are intended to be read as a source of interesting information, not as medical advice. Do not attempt self-treatment without seeking the professional advice of a qualified herbalist.

C O N T E N T S

ACKNOWLEDGEMENTS

Gerasimos Razis-Galiatsatos for his help and the illustrations which have made this book possible.
Constantine Staveris, Director of the Ecclesiastical Byzantine Museum, St Andrew's Monastery, Cephalonia, for his advice regarding local customs.
Several kind friends for their editorial comments, especially Father John Mesoloras and Anghelos Phocas.

Maria Micheletti and Yorgos Georgiou for the loan of a computer and warm hospitality.
And finally, my mother, father and sister for their loving help and encouragement.

Thank you.

St George's Castle

FOREWORD

This book written by Anna Maria Simpson seeks to increase the reader's enjoyment of the wild herbs and trees of Cephalonia by relating them to our historical background and traditions. The author brings together the medicinal and culinary uses of wild plants together with culture and mythology. The way she treats the subject is imbued with her love for nature and the customs of our island.

The text is enlivened by the very attractive drawings by Gerasimos Razis-Galiatsatos and many quotations.

This interesting book is not only informative but also a voice awaking us to the beauty and importance of elements which day by day are vanishing from our lives.

CONSTANTINE STAVERIS
Director of the Ecclesiastical Byzantine Museum

View of the port of Argostoli

And God said, Behold, I have given you every herb bearing seed, which is upon the face of all the earth, and every tree, in which is the fruit of a tree yielding seed; to you it shall be for meat.

Genesis, 1.29

INTRODUCTION

Cephalonia is an island of great natural beauty. Its high mountains and fertile valleys are richly endowed with plants. Close to its dramatic sea shores thrive many sweet scented wild herbs. Although two and a half thousand years separate us from ancient times, this book attempts to link some of the herbs and trees of the island to Greece's distant past by way of plant lore, mythology, literature and illustrations.

In parts of the island today, some of the trusted herbal remedies that have been passed down through the centuries continue to be used. There is still a rich tradition of using flowers, leaves and herbs in local customs and religious celebrations. The main festivals have been listed at the back of the book.

The illustrator and I hope that the reader will enjoy Cephalonia's magnificent landscape with its wealth of nature and that this small book will give pleasure.

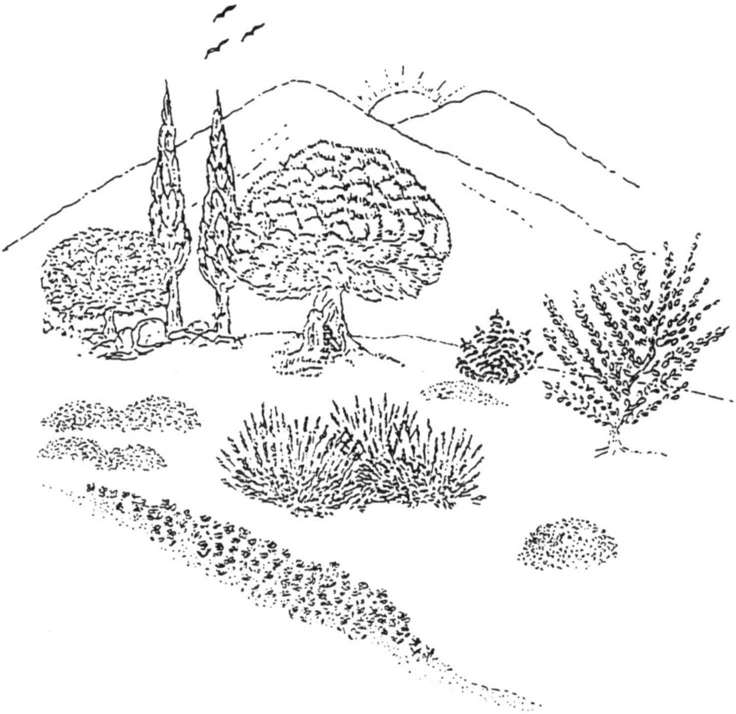

All Nature, is like one single apothecary's shop,
Covered only by the roof of Heaven....
PARACELSUS, 16th century

MEDICINES OUT OF THE EARTH

From the earliest times plants have been used medicinally. Their power to heal the ailments of mankind and his fellow creatures is well known.

People of ancient cultures lived close to nature and were more attuned to the earth and its rhythms. Plants were of great significance in the daily lives of the ancient Greeks and occupied an important place in mythology, art and religious ceremonies. In those distant days, medicinal herbs were believed to be gifts from the gods. Asclepius was known as the god of medicine and healing and was worshipped throughout Greece. Sanctuaries dedicated to him were always built in beautiful places conducive to healing. They were found close to fresh water springs, on high mountains, in shady forests, beside cool rivers and overlooking the sea.

In the 5th century BC, Hippocrates founded a school of natural healing on the island of Kos. He was to free medicine from mythological ideas linking health with the worship of gods. Asclepius, however, was not forgotten and Hippocrates and his followers named their group after him. Asclepius was depicted in most statues dressed in a long cloak, holding a staff entwined with a sacred snake. The snake was an ancient sign of wisdom, renovation and healing. The emblem of the staff with the snake is often seen nowadays and still signifies medicine and healing.

The success that Greek doctors had in ancient times was known throughout the Mediterranean region and their knowledge of medical science was eventually to reach the whole civilized world.

In Europe, during the middle ages, the monasteries translated and copied the ancient texts. They cultivated extensive herb gardens and recorded the use and effects of plants. Eventually, information regarding medicinal herbs spread from the monasteries, and with the invention of the printing press in the 15th century numerous herbals began to be produced. Classical knowledge was combined with simple household remedies that had been passed down from generation to generation.

Many of the medicinal plants described by the ancient Greeks are still in use. An example of the long-lasting influence of plant lore from classical Greece was observed by a director of the Royal Botanic Gardens at Kew when he visited Mount Athos (the Holy Mountain of northern Greece) in 1934. He and two other botanists were collecting plants there and happened to meet an official botanist, a herbalist monk. They were interested and impressed to see the monk at work collecting plants of medicinal value. He travelled swiftly over the peninsula on foot and sometimes on a mule for longer journeys. On his back he carried a large bag containing his “flora” which consisted of four volumes in manuscript copied from Dioscorides.[1] When the English botanists asked him the name of a plant that they were unfamiliar with, the monk promptly opened his bag and from one of the volumes he pointed out the identification of the plant.

In Cephalonia herbs are found growing in places of outstanding beauty. It is interesting to note that the sweet fragrance emanating from a herb is often closely associated with its healing properties and can actually add to our sense of wellbeing.

---

1. Ancient Greeks referred to in the text are listed in the appendix

The Lord hath created medicines out of the earth;
and he that is wise will not abhor them.
Ecclesiastes, 38.4

You know the appointed end of all things and all the ways.
You know how many leaves the earth unfolds in the spring,
how many grains of sand are driven by storm wind and wave
in the rivers and the sea.

PINDAR, 5th century BC

Acanthus Spiny Bear's Breech (*Ácanthos*)

A handsome plant with stately spikes of flowers and spiny leaves. It is native to the Mediterranean and was popular in the gardens of the ancient Greeks. In the 5th century BC, a sculptor called Callimachus observed an acanthus plant growing around a vase on a tomb in Corinth. Its graceful foliage inspired him to invent the leafy capital seen on Corinthian columns of classical Greek buildings. Its decorative leaves were used frequently in art.

According to Dioscorides the roots were used medicinally for a number of ailments, including ruptures and convulsions. Pliny the Elder, the natural historian of the 1st century AD, refers to a preparation of acanthus leaves for bruises. The leaves can be useful today. They may be crushed and applied to minor burns to bring relief.

In spring, soft young acanthus leaves are eaten by Cephalonians. The leaves are boiled together with other wild edible plants.

Acanthus spinosus
Tall perennial with stiff green leaves and whitish spines. Stout stem carrying numerous white flowers with purple veins. Grows to a height of 1m. Meadows, shady places and roadsides. Flowers: May-June

They passed the streams of Ocean the White Rock, the gates of the Sun and the land of dreams and soon they came to the field of asphodel, where the souls, the spirits of the dead, dwell.

Odyssey 24.10. HOMER, 8th century BC

Asphodel *(Asphódelos)*

This tall elegant plant was used medicinally by the ancient Greeks. Dioscorides mentions that it was employed for hernias, convulsions, coughs and toothache. The bruised root was used for swellings.

In ancient times asphodels were eaten when there was a scarcity of food. Theophrastus tells us that the stalk was fried and the seeds roasted. The root was considered to be very nutritious and often roasted together with figs.

Asphodels were often to be found near graves as the roots were regarded as nourishment for the spirits of the dead. Many ancient poems refer to this custom. In mythology these plants graced the "Elysian fields", the land of the blessed in the underworld where the heroes and sons of gods dwelt.

Asphodels may be seen growing in profusion in the Cephalonian countryside in springtime. They are much disliked by goats and sheep.

Asphodelus aestivus
Strong perennial with rush-like leaves growing low on the ground. Branched leafless stem, carrying pretty delicate flowers daintily striped with pinkish brown. Grows to a height of about 1.40m. Found on open stony land and hillsides. Flowers: February-April (other species: *Asphodelus fistulosus*)

Sprigs of Borage are of known virtue to revive the hypochondriac and cheer the hard student.
JOHN EVELYN, 17th century

Borage *(Pourágino)*

Borage has always been associated with courage. It was said that borage was the famous *Nepenthés* of Homer. *Nepenthés* was a legendary potion that was believed to be uplifting. Pliny the Elder, the natural historian of the 1st century AD, wrote that the leaves and flowers in wine comforted the heart and made men and women glad and merry. The leaves were also believed to be good for the blood.

As the ancient Greeks pointed out, borage has an aroma reminiscent of cucumber. It is a useful culinary herb and in Cephalonia the leaves are often eaten in the winter and spring. They are cooked together with other edible wild plants. Young fresh borage leaves have a high concentration of vitamin C.

These days borage is used by herbalists for a number of ailments such as stress, nervous depression and respiratory problems. It may be also used as a soothing skin lotion. The oil extracted from the seeds is helpful for rheumatic and hormonal problems.

Borago officinalis
Branched annual with robust stem and wrinkly oval leaves. Bright sky blue star-shaped flowers clustered together and half nodding. Grows to about 75cm high.
Dry wild areas, cultivated ground and sometimes on the roadside.
Flowers: March-April

Pickled Capers

Gather and rinse enough capers to fill about 3/4 of a jar. Fill to the top with water and 20% salt. Cap well and shake occasionally to disperse the salt. Change the salty water every 24 hours for 2 days. Rinse and place capers in a jar of apple vinegar. They are soft and ready to eat after about 3 weeks.

Caper *(Cápari)*

An attractive climbing plant which was well known to the ancient Greeks. The stalks, buds and fruit were preserved in salt and highly valued as a vegetable as well as a flavouring. The Greek poet and playwright Antiphanes included capers, thyme, sesame, cumin, marjoram, vinegar and olives in his list of seasonings. Athenaeus mentions capers on six occasions in his famous book "The Learned Banquet". Dioscorides tells us that the plant was used for various ailments including sciatica, swellings and toothache. Galen employed the powdered root mixed with honey and vinegar for treating the spleen. In the 4th century AD, it is known that the famous Greek doctor Orivasius prescribed capers for intestinal problems.

Capers (the unopened buds) are considered to be a tonic for the digestive system. In many countries, capers are a popular addition to salads and sauces.

Capparis spinosa
Spiny shrub with delicate white, sometimes pinkish, flowers and oval leaves. May grow to a height of 2m. Found climbing over ruins, dry slopes and rocky places near the sea shore. Flowers: May-July (other species: *Capparis orientalis*)

To see a World in a Grain of Sand
And a Heaven in a Wild Flower,
Hold Infinity in the palm of your hand
And Eternity in an hour.
WILLIAM BLAKE, 18th century

Chamomile *(Chamomíli)*

This sweet scented herb with its delicate little white flowers has a distinct smell of apple and was given the name "ground apple" by the ancient Greeks. Chamomile takes its name from the Greek words *hamaí*, on the ground and *mílon*, apple. It was well known in ancient times for its healing properties and was recommended by Dioscorides as a treatment for fevers, headaches and illnesses affecting the liver.

In Greece today, chamomile is a popular and well loved herb. It is picked in the early summer when the moon is on the wane, dried and used throughout the year as tea. This herb is soothing and sleep-inducing due to its sedative properties and is helpful for stomach problems and indigestion. An infusion of chamomile flowers can be used for toothache and certain skin problems. Employed as a final rinse for blonde hair it has a lightening effect.

In folklore chamomile was known as "the plant's physician" since it can promote the health of plants growing nearby.

Matricaria Chamomilla
Annual with tiny daisy-like flowers and dainty feathery leaves. Grows up to 50cm.
Flourishes in dry sandy soil, in wide open land and grassy places.
Flowers: April–May

By Hera, this is a beautiful place for a rest. The plane tree here is spreading and very tall, and the agnos (chaste-tree) is splendidly high and shady and in full bloom, filling the area with the finest fragrance.

PLATO, 5th century BC

Chaste-Tree Monk's pepper (*Ligariá*)

In ancient Greece, chaste tree was one of the most highly regarded herbs. Its name *ágnos* in Greek and *cástus* in Latin both mean chaste. Dioscorides recorded that matrons lay on couches prepared with this herb to affirm their chastity at festivals held in honour of Demeter, the goddess of the harvest.

Chaste-tree was also associated with Hera, the goddess of marriage. In the 1st century AD, according to Pausanias, a very old chaste-tree decorated the entrance to a temple dedicated to Hera on the island of Samos.

Today this plant is used medicinally for treating female hormonal disorders. In Greek folk medicine the berries are known to be a female aphrodisiac. However, chaste-tree is also known to be a male anaphrodisiac and was used as such in medieval times.

Vitex agnus-castus
Large deciduous shrub with deeply-cut dark green leaves. Spikes of sweet-scented tiny flowers varying from lilac to pink or blue. Grows up to 6m.
Gullies, ditches and damp places near the sea. Flowers: July-August

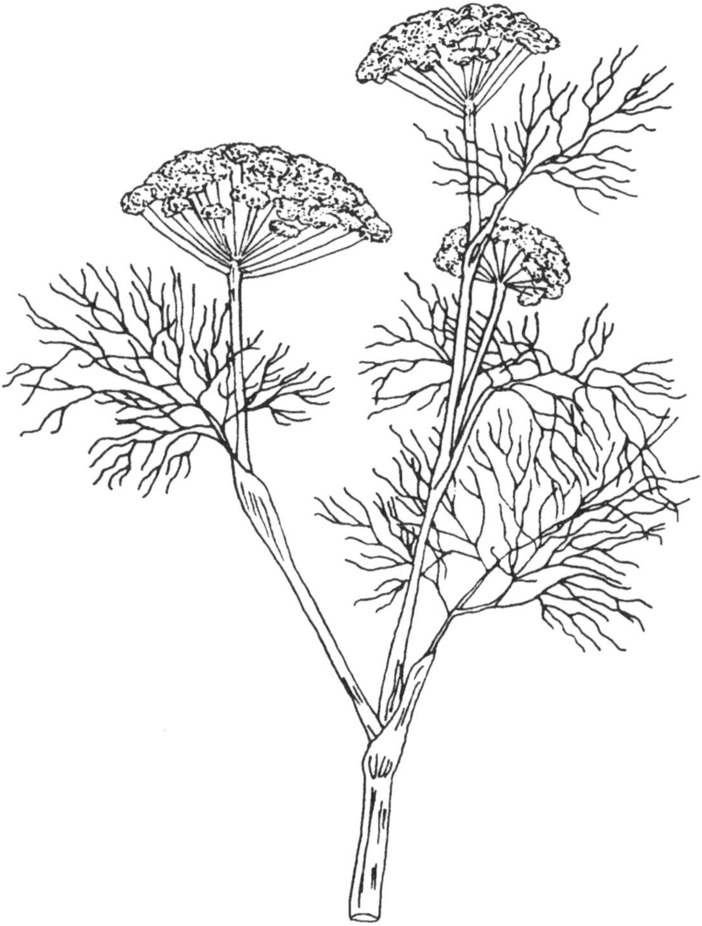

Above the lowly plants it towers,
The fennel, with its yellow flowers,
And in an age earlier than ours
Was gifted with the wondrous powers,
Lost vision to restore.

LONGFELLOW, 19th century

Fennel *(Máratho)*

This graceful aromatic herb takes its Greek name from the word *maraínome,* to grow thinner. It is known that athletes allayed hunger and kept slim by chewing the seeds and eating the shoots. It was believed that fennel conveyed longevity and gave strength and courage. It was also thought to have a strange strengthening effect on the eyesight.

In mythology, the hero Prometheus secretly stole fire from heaven. He hid the fire in the hollow stem of a giant fennel and brought it back to earth for mankind. During the Dionysian festivals the attendants of Dionysus, the god of wine, each carried a wand made out of a large fennel stalk topped with a pine cone called a thyrsus. Fennel was used instead of wood because if, under the influence of wine, they had a quarrel they were unlikely to injure themselves.

Today, this herb is used medicinally for indigestion and respiratory problems and is also effective as an eye wash. The essential oil, distilled from the seeds, is helpful in the treatment of obesity and rheumatism. In Cephalonia fennel is used in cooking and used to be an important ingredient for liqueurs.

Foeniculum vulgare
Perennial, indigenous to the shores of the Mediterranean, with thick hollow stems that look almost polished. Feathery bright green leaves and deep golden flowers. Grows up to 2.5m or more in height. Dry hillsides and sandy or rocky places often near the sea. Flowers: June-July

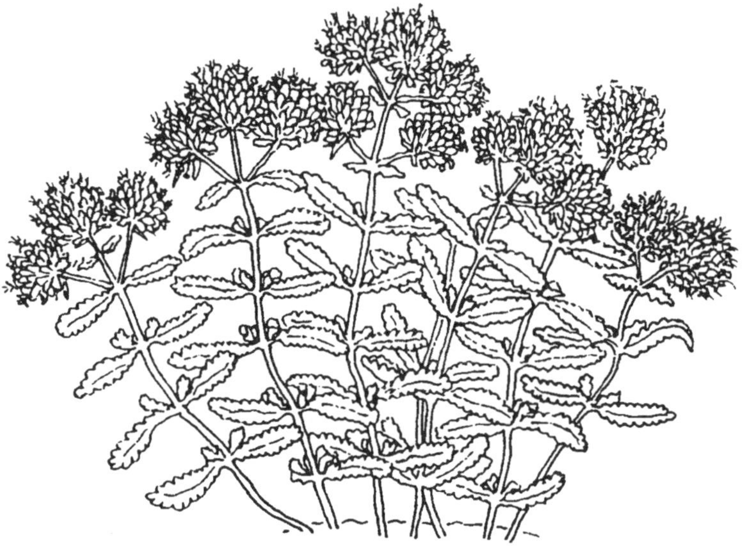

There is no creation
that does not have a radiance
be it greenness of seed
blossom or beauty.

HILDEGARD OF BINGEN, 12th century

Felty Germander *(Panagióhorto)*

This small felty herb with its distinctive fragrance was esteemed by the ancient Greeks for its medicinal properties. There are many descriptions regarding the use of germander. It was believed to be a general remedy. Dioscorides recommended it for stomach aches, fevers and colds. Germander was used in wine as a remedy for jaundice and it was also considered to be a diuretic. Hesiod, the ancient Greek poet, suggested that germander should be cultivated and carried at all times as a remedy for snake bites and various other poisons. The plant's Latin name comes from Teucer, an ancient king of Troy, who was said to be the first to use this herb medicinally.

The common Greek name for felty germander is *Panagióhorto,* "herb of the Virgin Mary", which tells us how much this herb was treasured. In Greece today it is employed for diabetes, digestive disorders, coughs and colds. It is also regarded as a general tonic.

Teucrium polium
Dwarf shrub with small narrow, toothed leaves. White or pale pink flowers. Grows up to 15-30cm. Dry rocky or stony places and in open forest.
Flowers: June-July (There are several species.)

...... a decoction of it like Hyssop is good for distress in the thorax.
It is mingled also profitably with antidotes.

DIOSCORIDES, lst century AD

.... especially good for all griefs and pains of the head and brain.

JOHN PARKINSON, l7th century

Lavender *(Levánda)*

Amongst life's more simple pleasures must surely be the sight of this exquisite herb growing wild in the mountains. Lavender, with its dainty purple flowers, has always been cherished for its sweet fragrance and valuable healing properties. Its name is derived from the Latin *lavare,* to wash, and it was often used for cleansing wounds.

Lavender was well known by the ancient Greeks for its calming and uplifting properties. It was used as incense. The water they bathed in was often scented with lavender, and the oil was used for massage. This aromatic herb was also employed as an insect repellent.

Today, lavender may be used as a tea for certain ailments such as fainting, headaches and sunstroke. The essential oil is particularly good for easing muscular pain, healing burns and for treating headaches, stress and insomnia. A drop of oil on an insect bite can bring relief.

In some villages in Cephalonia, they make neat little bundles of lavender for scenting and protecting clothes and linen, and young boys are often found selling them outside the Monastery of St Gerasimos in summer.

Lavandula angustifolia

Woody shrub with narrow greyish-green leaves and bluish-purple flowers growing in spikes. Grows to a height of 80cm. High up on stony hill sides and in the mountains. Flowers: June–July

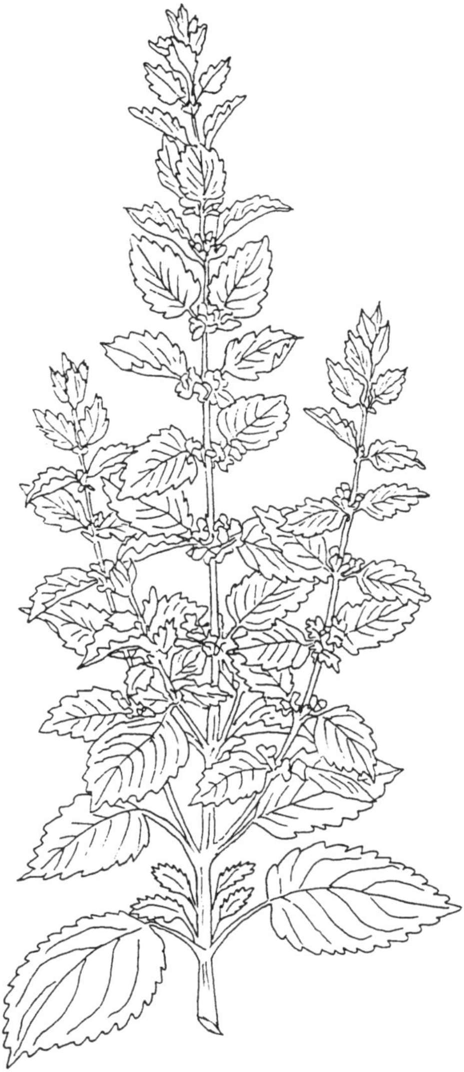

Balm, being applied, doth close up wounds without any peril of inflammation.
DIOSCORIDES, 1st century AD

Lemon Balm (*Melissóchorto or Melissovótano*)

Lemon balm's official name *Mélissa* is the Greek word for honey bee. Bees are attracted to this plant and it has been used to lure them to a new hive. In ancient Greece, lemon balm was used for anxiety and melancholia and for healing gout, wounds and insect bites. It was considered to be sacred and was used in the temples of Artemis, the goddess of the moon and the hunt.

This herb, with its lemon-scented aroma, was an important ingredient in medieval cordials and was said to fortify the heart. Paracelsus, a 16th century physician, called it "the elixir of life". Later, in the 18th century it was believed that lemon balm could renew youth.

In herbal medicine today lemon balm is generally employed for its calming and uplifting properties. It is helpful for tension and depression and excellent for digestive problems due to anxiety. It can bring relief to painful swellings and sores. Fresh lemon balm leaves may be applied to insect bites and stings.

Tea made from this herb has a delicate lemon flavour and is still enjoyed by the people of Cephalonia. An infusion of the fresh leaves used to be valued as a rinse for greasy hair.

Melissa officinalis

Branched perennial with soft serrated bright green leaves and tiny white or pink flowers. Grows to a height of 1m or more.

Ditches and damp shady places. Flowers: June-July

....whoever swallows daily half a cyathus of the juice of any one of the mallows will be immune to all diseases that may come to him.

PLINY THE ELDER, 1st century AD

Common Mallow (*Molócha*)

The name of this herb is derived from the Greek word *malakós,* meaning soft. Mallow has special qualities and is able to soften and heal. It was an important medicinal herb in ancient times. Dioscorides recommended its use for bruises, inflammation of the skin and as a protection from stings and bites. Early classical writers mention that the leaves, roots and flowers were all eaten. Mallow was an important vegetable for the poor.

In herbal medicine today mallow is still highly valued, especially the root. It can promote the healing of internal injuries and is very helpful in cases of stomach ulcers and gastritis. It may be used for respiratory disorders and for certain skin conditions.

In Cephalonia tea made from the flowers is a popular remedy for sore throats, coughs and stomach complaints. Dried mallow flowers may be found in the market in Argostoli during the summer. When dried, the little flowers are a deep bluish-purple.

Malva sylvestris

Hairy biennial or perennial with heart-shaped leaves and pink or purple flowers with dark veins. Grows up to a height of 2.5m. Meadows, open land and roadsides. Flowers: March-May (There are several species.)

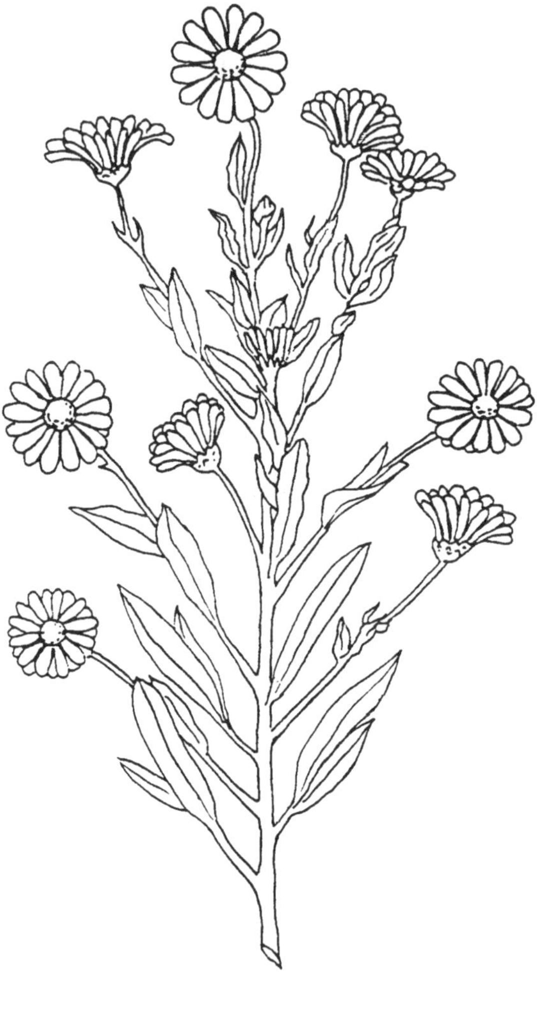

A conserve made of the flowers and sugar, taken in the morning fasting, cureth the trembling of the heart, and is also given in the time of plague or pestilence.

STEVENS, 17th century

Field Marigold *(Caléndoula)*

A herb of ancient medical repute which was said to be in bloom for each month of the Roman calendar, hence its Latin name. In the middle ages it was believed that simply looking at the golden flowers of marigold cleared the head, strengthened the eyesight and brought cheer.

Marigold is traditionally known in herbal medicine to be one of the best healers. It is highly antiseptic and is an exceptional herb for treating skin problems. It can reduce inflammation and help in the healing of bruises, burns and wounds. It is also soothing for the digestive system. The sap from the stem has a reputation for curing warts and corns. This herb deserves a place in every medicine chest!

Field marigold grows in many places in Cephalonia and to come across these bright little flowers lighting up grassy areas is indeed a joyful sight.

Calendula arvensis

Annual with oblong leaves, straggly stems and small yellow flowers. Grows to a height of 50cm. ✐ Olive groves, vineyards, fields, grassy places and waste land. Flowers: October-April

And finally, it is good for ye stomach, and fit for sauce.

DIOSCORIDES, 1st century AD

Mint (*Ménta*)

Mint takes its name from Greek mythology. Minthe was a nymph much loved by Hades, the god of the underworld. His wife, Persephone, was very jealous of Minthe and transformed her into the plant we now call mint.

In classical times people believed mint to be strengthening and refreshing. It was added to the water they bathed in and valued for its cool, sweet fragrance. Crowns were made of mint and worn at feasts. It was also used for culinary purposes and for decoration. The sacred cup given to Demeter, the goddess of the harvest, and her followers at Eleusis contained barley water flavoured with mint. Today it is traditional to flavour *spermá* (see p. 94) with mint.

In herbal medicine, mint is best known as a remedy for indigestion. It may also be used for nausea, travel sickness and headaches. It can help to reduce a fever and is useful for treating respiratory infections and relieving muscular pain. In Cephalonia, especially in the villages, mint tea is still popular and appreciated for its refreshing and digestive qualities.

Mentha spicata
Perennial herb with green leaves and spikes of pale lilac flowers. Grows to a height of 40cm. Damp shady areas, sometimes in more open grassy places. Flowers: May-June (There are several species.)

....beasts of burden that are not only suffering from cough
but also broken-winded, are relieved by a draught.

PLINY THE ELDER, 1st century AD

Mullein *(Melissaroú)*

In classical times the tall stems of mullein were set alight and carried in funeral processions. This herb was important medicinally and was employed for coughs and colds. Dioscorides mentions its use for treating ulcers, scorpion stings and toothache. It was possibly mullein that Odysseus took from Hermes, the messenger of the gods, to protect himself against the spells of a beautiful and dangerous witch called Circe. In those days it was believed that this plant had such powers.

Today herbalists still use both the flowers and the leaves of mullein for respiratory problems. The leaves used to be made into herbal tobacco and smoked for asthma and tuberculosis. An infused oil made from the flowers can be employed for ear-ache and certain skin problems.

Mullein, with its tall spires of yellow flowers, may be found growing in large colonies in the countryside; it is avoided by grazing sheep and goats.

Verbascum densiflorum

Biennial with large felty grey-green leaves and thick stem. Sulphur-yellow flowers. It may reach a height of 1.5m. Open stony areas, hillsides and near roads. Flowers: May-June (There are several species.)

The herb being strewn on the ground repels snakes.
DIOSCORIDES, 1st century AD

Oregano *(Rígani)*

This herb's name derives from two ancient Greek words *óros,* mountain and *gános,* splendour. Accordingly, oregano was known as "splendour of the mountains" and it certainly is a delightful sight to see this aromatic herb in full bloom on the sun-drenched hillsides in summer.

In ancient Greece warm poultices were made from the leaves and used for painful swellings. Oregano was also a remedy for toothache, digestive upsets and respiratory problems. Today it is still considered helpful for the digestion and continues to be used to relieve toothache.

Oregano has always been used for culinary purposes. Traditionally, you should always find oregano on the famous Greek "village salad", *horiátiki saláta.* In Cephalonia *riganátha (*dry bread dipped in water, covered with olive oil, vinegar, tomato, salt and a generous sprinkling of oregano) used to be a tasty, practical picnic lunch for shepherds and workers on the land. Today when the tomatoes are ripe and sweet, *riganátha* is still made in the villages. A simple meal made from local produce, when shared with wine, can be as enjoyable as any feast.

Origanum heracleoticum

Perennial with thin wiry stem and small oval leaves growing in pairs. Flowers are pinkish or white and hop-like. Grows to a height of 50cm.

Dry stony places, hillsides and mountains. Flowers: June

There's rosemary, that's for remembrance....
SHAKESPEARE, 16th century

...smell it often and it will keep thee young.
BANCKES' HERBAL, 16th century

Rosemary *(Dendrolívanon)*

An attractive evergreen herb with a strong refreshing fragrance. It is surrounded by tradition and legend. Its Greek name *dendrolívanon* means "incense tree". Rosemary was often employed as incense in religious ceremonies, and statues of the gods were garlanded with it. Rosemary was said to be a gift to mankind from Aphrodite, the goddess of love and beauty. Since ancient times it has been used as a culinary and medicinal herb. Scholars used to twine a rosemary sprig in their hair while they were studying because it was believed to strengthen the memory. This herb became a symbol of fidelity and remembrance.

Today, rosemary is known for its invigorating and stimulating properties. It is an excellent tonic and valuable for respiratory problems. The essential oil is most helpful for pains in the muscles and joints. An infusion of rosemary leaves can be used as a tonic for dark hair. In Cephalonia, rosemary is valued as a remedy for headaches. It is also used in cooking.

Rosmarinus officinalis

Evergreen shrub with small narrow leaves, green above and white below. Small pale mauve flowers. Grows to a height of 1.5m. Rocky areas near the sea, dry hill sides and scrubland. Flowers: intermittantly throughout the year

Why should a man die whilst Sage grows in his garden.
Roman, anon

Sage (*Faskómilo*)

Sage was said to guarantee a long life and has been esteemed for its healing powers since antiquity. The Latin name *Salvia* is derived from a word meaning salvation. Sage was used by all the ancient doctors. It was also appreciated as incense and for its culinary uses.

Sage is still used medicinally today for many of the same complaints that it was prescribed for in the past - respiratory problems, sore throats, rheumatism, digestive ailments and wounds. It also has the ability to stimulate the memory. It was recorded in herbals of the 16th century that sage was particularly good for the head and brain and quickened the senses.

In Cephalonia sage tea is considered a useful remedy for colds, coughs, headaches and stomach upsets. People collect sage apples (galls) to eat when they are juicy and sweet in the early summer. This attractive shrub with its warm, spicy scent is a familiar sight on the island.

Salvia fruticosa

Shrub with soft velvety greyish-green leaves, often with a pair of small lobes. Pink, lilac or white flowers. Grows to a height of 1.5m. Rocky places, stony pastures, hillsides and mountains. Flowers: March-May (There are several species.)

The fig progresses more quickly and is less eaten by grubs if the cutting is set in a sea squill bulb. In fact, anything so planted is vigorous and grows faster.

THEOPHRASTUS, 3rd century BC

Sea Squill *(Ayiovasilítsa)*

The sea squill was valued highly as a medicinal plant in ancient times. For Hippocrates and his followers it was an important herb for disorders of the lungs and for the treatment of jaundice. *Oxýmeli* of squill (squill together with vinegar and honey) was invented by Pythagoras and was widely used as a cough medicine. This powerful herb is still employed by herbalists for respiratory problems.

The sea squill is considered to be the sea onion mentioned by Homer. It looks like a very large onion shallowly embedded in the soil and often appearing above the ground. It survives the hot dry summers and with the first autumn rains produces a tall spike of delicate white starry flowers.

This plant was associated with purity and fertility. The ancient Greeks used to hang a sea squill bulb over the doorway of the house. It symbolised the life force they wanted to bestow on the house and family and it was believed to ward off evil spirits. This ancient custom survives to this day (see p.104).

Urginea maritima
Short perennial with an extremely large bulb, shiny green leaves and white flowers on a tall stem. Grows to a height of lm. Found often in colonies, on rocky hillsides and in dry sandy places. Flowers: September

---

*The squill retains its life force for a long time. It was reported in England in the 19th century that a bulb was found attempting to grow after being stowed away for more than twenty years in the museum of St Bartholomew's Hospital Medical School.

And the seed being drunk for forty days cures sciatica ....

DIOSCORIDES, 1st century AD

St John's Wort *(Valsamóchorto)*

This graceful herb with its golden flowers was held in high esteem by the ancient Greeks. It had a reputation for warding off evil which may have been due to its wide range of medicinal uses. St John's Wort was used as a remedy for wounds. According to Dioscorides, it was an antidote to snake bites.

It takes its English name from the Knights of St John of Jerusalem who, during the Crusades, used it on the battlefields for treating sword wounds. This versatile herb is still widely employed in medical herbalism. It has the ability to alleviate the pain of sciatica, neuralgia and arthritis. It is most helpful in the treatment of anxiety and depression and is useful in healing gastritis and stomach ulcers. It is also very soothing for burns.

People still collect St John's wort in Cephalonia. A glass jar filled with fresh flowers and olive oil is left in the sunlight for two or three weeks until the oil becomes a rich ruby red colour. It is then used for skin complaints.

Hypericum perfoliatum
Perennial with small oval to pointed leaves and yellow flowers. Grows up to 50cm.
Quiet undisturbed places, dry hillsides and near trees in stony meadows.
Flowers: April-May (there are several species)

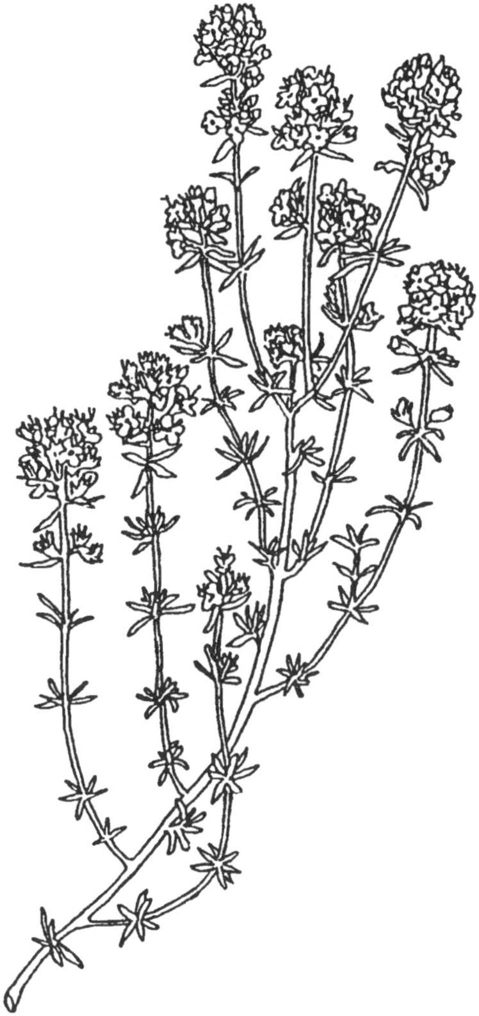

A decoction of it with honey helps breathing problems and asthma, and it expels worms ....

DIOSCORIDES, 1st century AD

Thyme (*Thimári*)

The name of this strongly aromatic herb originates from the Greek word *thimió,* to burn incense. Thyme was used by the ancient Greeks in religious ceremonies. It was employed medicinally and was thought of as invigorating and inspiring courage. Thyme was appreciated as a perfume. It was also used as a disinfectant and as a preservative.

Today, thyme is mostly used for chills, respiratory complaints and digestive problems, and in preventing and treating infection. It is one of nature's best herbal antiseptics.

Bees have a remarkable instinct for medicinal herbs. They will choose the tiny aromatic flowerlets of thyme, rosemary and lavender instead of grand flowers with easily attainable nectar. Cephalonia is famous for its thyme honey, *méli thimarísio,* which has a fine rich flavour and since ancient times has been considered a luxury. Pure thyme honey can also heal a minor wound.

In Cephalonia people still wisely make thyme tea for colds and coughs, and some chew this herb to keep the teeth healthy. During the vintage, a broom of thyme is made for cleaning the stone *linós* used for treading the grapes. In summer a tasty aromatic cheese called *préntza* is made in the villages. *Préntza* is soft white cheese made from goat's or sheep's milk mixed together with fresh wild thyme.

Thymus capitatus

Shrub with tiny stiff leaves and woody stems.Very small purplish-pink flowers. Grows to a height of 40cm. Rocky places near the sea, dry hillsides and mountains. Flowers: June-July

Joy in music of flutes
Joy when sparkling wine at feasts of the gods,
Soothes the sore regret
Banishes every grief....
EURIPIDES, 5th century BC

Indeed, I think life is at its best when there is tranquillity among the people and banqueters in the palace, sitting next to each other, listen to a singer, while the tables in front of them are laden with bread and meat, and a servant brings sweet wine from brimming bowls and fills their cups. This seems to me, in my heart, to be the most joyful thing of all.
Odyssey 9.5. HOMER, 8th century BC

CULINARY HERBS

From literature, pottery and other archaeological finds we are able to understand what the ancient Greeks ate and drank. At a banquet the air was scented and the guests were presented with perfumed oils and wreaths of fragrant flowers and leaves. The meals were lavish and often one dish would contain as many as three or four herbs. Many of the herbs would have been available in the garden. The following herbs are known to have been used in the kitchens of classical Greece: capers, bay berries, coriander, cumin, dill, fennel, garlic, hyssop, lovage, mint, mustard, oregano, parsley, pennyroyal, rue, sage and wormwood.

Today, each region of Greece has its own special dishes and various ways of using herbs. In Cephalonia, the herbs that grow so freely on the island are often used in the seasoning of food. They include: bay, dill, fennel, garlic, marjoram, mint, oregano, parsley, rosemary and thyme.

Since ancient times Greek people have been very enthusiastic about eating *ágria hórta*, wild greens (edible weeds). In times of hardship they were a vital part of the diet. Today, from autumn until early spring, it is still a popular pastime to go out into the countryside and gather *hórta*. Many of the older women in Cephalonia can identify all the different kinds of wild greens and take pleasure in choosing which to collect. They also understand the health benefits from eating them. In the past, most people in Europe would have been familiar with wild edible plants.

In the Saturday open-air market of Argostoli, it is fascinating to see wooden tables piled high with freshly picked wild greens and herbs such as borage, chicory, common sow thistle, crown daisy, dandelion, dill, dock, fennel, wild garlic, wild leek, common hedge mustard, nettle, nipplewort, field poppy leaves, plantain, shepherd's needle, wild carrot, parsley and tordylium.

Three dishes are made from these wild plants - *hórta (*boiled wild greens served with olive oil and lemon), the famous *hortópitta (*a pie made with wild greens and aromatic herbs) and *tsigarídia (*wild greens cooked with aromatic herbs, oil and tomato).

Wild asparagus, black bryony shoots and common grape hyacinth are also collected for eating and can be found in the market in springtime. In the summer purslane grows in many areas, and in the autumn rock samphire is found along the seashores. They are both used for salads.

Let your food be your medicine.

HIPPOCRATES, 4th century BC

Tsigarídia

Ingredients:

A mixture (about 1 kg.) of shepherd's needle, tordylium, field poppy leaves, borage, dock leaves, chard, spinach and nettles.

Aromatic herbs: A small bunch of marjoram, wild leeks, fennel, dill, wild garlic (or several cloves of garlic). 1 or 2 tablespoons of olive oil, two fresh tomatoes or 1 full teaspoon of tomato puree mixed in about 50ml of water. Pinch of salt and pepper.

Cut all the vegetables into small pieces. Cook the mixture of wild plants (with the lid on) turning them over until they soften a little (about 10 mins). Squeeze all the liquid out. Add the aromatic herbs, oil, tomato and seasoning. Cook gently until ready (about 40 mins). If the vegetables begin to stick to the pan add a little water.

View of Mount Aenos from the sea

Odysseus then commanded the brave men of Cephalonia
who had Ithaca and leafy Niritos
and they lived at Krokylia and rugged Aegilips, and they had Zakinthos
and Samos and the coast of the mainland with its opposing isles;
Odysseus, peer of Zeus in wisdom, led them in twelve good ships
with scarlet painted sides.

Iliad 2.734. HOMER, 8th century BC

THE TREES OF THE LAND

.....and the leaves of the tree were for the healing of the nations.
Revelation, 22. 2

Trees are an integral part of creation and essential to our life. They have continually supplied the needs of mankind, and the healing qualities of trees have been valued through the ages.
In ancient times a great part of Greece was forested. Woodland was the primary feature of the Homeric landscape. Enormous quantities of wood were used for building, especially in the construction of ships.

The traditions, history and colourful legends associated with trees can be inspiring. In Greek mythology the trees were associated with nymphs and gods; the saying "touch wood" comes from those distant times when trees were thought to give good luck and spiritual strength. In the 1st century AD the natural historian Pliny the Elder wrote....

Trees were once the temples of the divine powers and following traditional ritual, simple country people still dedicate a tree that is particularly grand to a god. Nor do we honour with our worship wooden images gleaming with gold and ivory more than sacred groves and their silence.

In Cephalonia there is a wide variety of trees of which a high proportion are evergreen and so the island remains verdant throughout the year. Whether the visitor arrives by air or sea, often the first glimpse of Cephalonia will be the distant view of the ancient, dark forest on the mountain of Aenos.

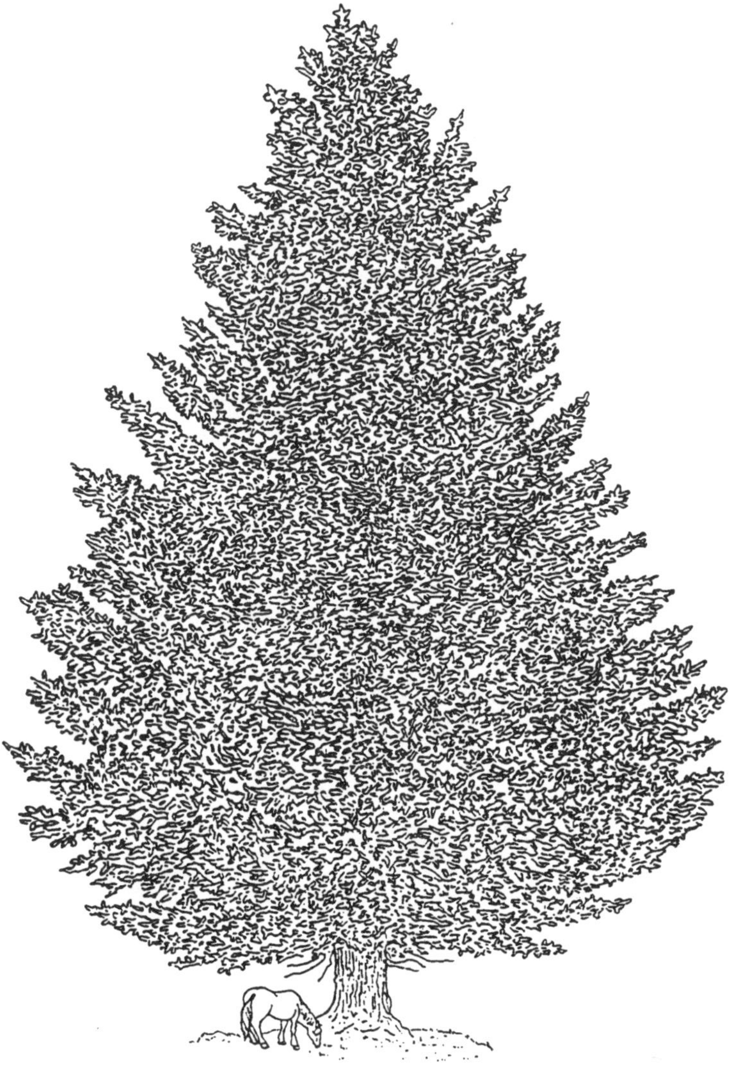

Fir trees, the tallest of trees grow heaven-high.

Odyssey 5.237. HOMER, 8th century BC

Cephalonian Fir Grecian Fir (*Élato*)

Cephalonians are justly proud of this magnificent tree which graces the slopes of the island's highest mountain, Mount Aenos. There was a time when the mountain was entirely covered by trees. Homer describes Cephalonia as *mélaina,* "the black one". From the sea the mountains must have appeared extremely dark due to this dense and extensive forest. The tall imposing fir tree was associated with Zeus, the father of gods and men, and on Mount Aenos there was once a temple dedicated to him.

The evergreen fir is mentioned many times in Homer's poems, even oars are simply referred to as "firs". It was the most useful timber for boat building and general construction. The columns of the ancient palace at Knossos in Crete were made from fir trees that were thought to have come from Cephalonia.

Icons, the religious paintings of the Orthodox Church, have through the centuries been painted on wooden panels made from of a variety of trees including fir.

In 1962 the forest of Aenos was declared a national park to give protection to this fine species of fir.

Abies cephalonica
Evergreen tree (growing in an altitude above 800m) with pyramidal crown. Tiny reddish flowers (May-June) and cylindrical erect cones (September-October). Grows to a height of 35m.
Mountains. Flourishes in an altitude of 800-1600m

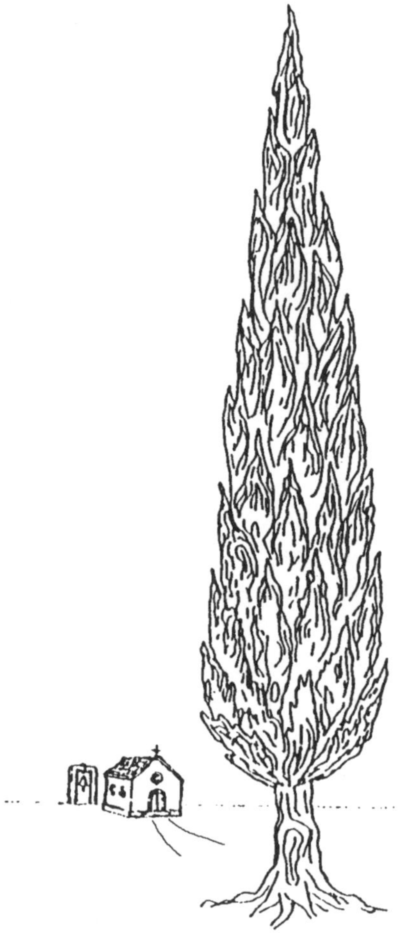

Oh! snatch'd away in beauty's bloom,
On thee shall press no ponderous tomb;
But on thy turf shall roses rear
Their leaves, the earliest of the year;
And the wild cypress wave in tender gloom:

LORD BYRON, 19th century

Cypress *(Cyparíssi)*

The cypress tree derives its name from an ancient Greek myth. Cyparissos was a young boy from Kea who was loved by Apollo, the god of light. Cyparissos had accidentally killed his cherished deer and his grief was so profound that he could not be consoled. In memory of his deep sadness, Apollo transformed him into a cypress tree.

In antiquity this tall dark tree was associated with death, sorrow and eternity. When someone died a branch was hung on the doorway of the house. The cypress has always been connected with cemeteries.* It is also known as "the Finger of God" because standing like a sentinel it points the way to Heaven. In Cephalonia this graceful tree is a principal feature of the island's landscape.

Cypress wood is very hard and long lasting and was used in the construction of ships and houses. Until recently, on some Greek islands, a cypress was planted when a daughter was born; it was part of her dowry and when she married it formed the mast for the wedded couple's boat.

Cupressus sempervirens

Evergreen tree with small, scale-like, dark green leaves. Flowers (January-March) and greyish round cones (July-August). Grows up to 30m or more. Hillsides, valleys, roadsides and near churches and monasteries.

*There are some fine examples of this tree, planted in the early 19th century, in the cemetery of Argostoli (across the bridge, 600m along the road to Assos). The 19th century British cemetery is in the same area (200 m after the bridge).

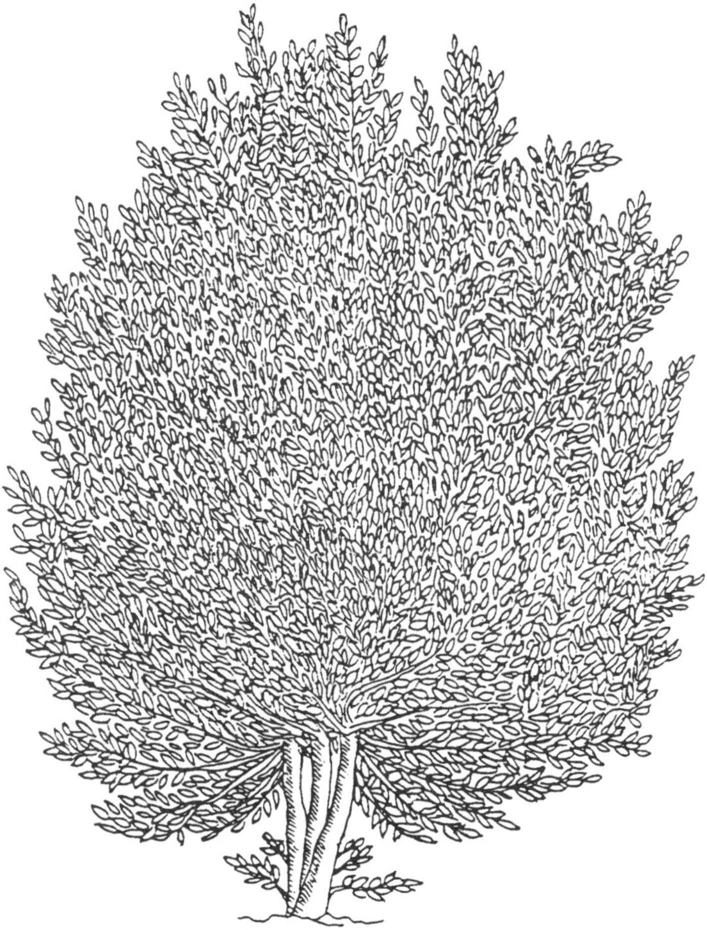

The gods, that mortal beauty chase,
Still in a tree did end their race.
Apollo hunted Daphne so,
Only that she might laurel grow.
And Pan did after Syrinx speed,
Not as a nymph, but for a reed.

ANDREW MARVELL, 17th century

Laurel Sweet Bay *(Dáphne)*

This aromatic tree takes its Greek name from a myth. Daphne was a beautiful mountain nymph loved by Apollo, the god of light and music. She was so distressed and overcome by Apollo's persistent advances that, in haste, she turned for help to Gaia, the goddess of the earth, who saved her by transforming her into a laurel. Apollo wore the leaves as a crown to remind himself of his beloved Daphne. When Apollo's oracle was consulted at Delphi, the responses were uttered by the Pythian priestess after chewing bay leaves and drinking from the sacred spring of Castalia.

The laurel became a symbol of respect, fame and victory. Its glossy dark green leaves were used for the crowns and wreaths of heroes and poets. In Greece today, the term "crowned with laurel" still signifies the greatest honour in the field of the arts and sports. Laurel was one of the scents most favoured by the ancient Greeks. Dioscorides recommended the oil as a general soothing remedy.

Today oil of bay is still used for strains and bruises. In Cephalonia not long ago, an oil made from the berries was used for protecting the skin of invalids. It was also used for smoothing and conditioning the hair.

Laurus nobilis
Evergreen shrub or small tree with shiny dark green leaves. Clusters of tiny yellow flowers (March-April) and small black berries (September). Grows to a height of 10m.
Dampish places, rocky areas and thickets.

*A tender child came bringing water for the hands in a silver ewer,
and poured it, then he brought a wreath plaited from the noble sprigs
of a slim Myrtle.*

PHILOXENUS, 4th century BC

Myrtle *(Mirtiá)*

In ancient Greece the myrtle tree was sacred to Aphrodite, the goddess of love and beauty. Myrtle with its aromatic, evergreen leaves, dainty white flowers and sweet scent was a symbol of love, peace and honour. It was often used for decorating temples and sanctuaries. Myrtle was used at the celebration of the sacred marriage between the god Zeus, the father of gods and humans, and Europa, daughter of Agenor, king of Tyre. The link between this plant and matrimony still exists today, myrtle flowers in a bridal crown signifying everlasting love.

An exquisite delicate 4th century BC gold myrtle wreath was discovered in 1977 in a royal tomb at Vergina, Macedonia. It is an object of exceptional beauty with 80 leaves and 112 flowers. Wreaths of myrtle were worn by magistrates, victors at the games and by guests at banquets. At banquets myrtle berries were chewed at the dessert time. In the autumn the fresh sweet berries are still enjoyed in Cephalonia.

Dioscorides prescribed myrtle for lung infections and it continues to be used for repiratory complaints today. Since ancient times essence of myrtle has been used in perfume making.

Myrtus communis
Small evergreen tree or bush. Dark pointed shiny leaves and small white flowers (June-July). Bluish-black berries (November). Grows to a height of about 3m.
Thickets, woods and scrubland.

Love again hath fluttered my heart, as a squall
That down from the hills on the oaks doth fall.

SAPPHO, 6th century BC

Oak *(Velanidiá)*

The majestic oak tree symbolised power and was associated with Zeus, the father of gods and men. At Dodona (north west Greece) there was a sacred oak tree where the people consulted him and his oracle was revealed by the rustling of the tree's leaves. The voice of Zeus also came in the form of thunder and lightning. The oak tree attracts lightning more than any other tree and for the ancient Greeks this was seen as a channel through which Zeus could reach down to them.

In ancient times a scarlet dye, only afforded by the rich, was obtained from the scale insect that lives on the leaves of the Kermes oak. From fragmented records of timber purchases that have survived we learn that oak was employed for building temples and for the construction of ships. Oak leaves were used for wreaths and connected with the worship of Dionysus, the god of wine.

Ripe acorns provide a rich harvest for woodland animals and in very early times they were also valued as food by man. Different parts of the tree have been used medicinally since ancient times. It is recorded that Galen applied the bruised leaves to heal wounds. Today oak bark is used by herbalists for treating gastric disorders and the leaves can promote the healing of certain skin conditions.

Kermes Oak (*Quercus coccifera*).
Evergreen tree or shrub with holly-like leaves and acorns in spiny cups (October-November). Flowers (April-May). Grows to a height of 2m and in the right conditions may grow into a large tree reaching a height of 20m. Stony ground and hillsides. Other species: Holm oak (*Quercus ilex*) and Downy oak (*Quercus pubescens*)

Well, there is in the Altis, when you are about to pass to the left of the Leonidaeum, an altar of Aphrodite, and after it one of the Seasons. About opposite the rear chamber a wild Olive is growing on the right. It is called the olive of the Beautiful Crown and from its leaves are made the crowns which it is customary to give to the winners of the Olympic contests.

PAUSANIAS, 2nd century AD

Olive *(Eliá)*

The olive tree is the most cherished of all trees in Greece. According to legend, there was a contest between Athena, the goddess of wisdom, and Poseidon, the god of the sea, for the possession of Attica. The gods had decided that the winner was to be the one who offered the most useful gift to the city. Athena was victorious, she created the first olive tree and the city of Athens was named after her. The olive tree, sacred to Athena, symbolised victory and peace.

The much prized oil was widely used for culinary purposes. It was also used as medicine, for anointing the body and in the making of perfumes and cosmetics.

Olive oil has always been a fundamental religious symbol in the liturgical life of the church. It symbolises the fullness of spiritual life - a gift of healing, peace and spiritual power. For thousands of years olive oil has been used as a source of light. In the church and in the homes oil lamps still give light to the icons.

The olive is the most widely cultivated tree in Cephalonia and there are some growing on the island today that are more than 2000 years old. Interestingly, methods of cultivation described by ancient authors are still in use. The production of olive oil has always been of considerable economic importance to the island. Olive oil continues to be a vital part of the Greek diet.

Olea europaea

Evergreen tree with grey-green leaves, silvery on the underside.Tiny clusters of white flowers (May). Oblong green fruit turning black when fully mature (November-January). Grows to a height of about 15m. Stony hillsides and groves outside villages. (There are several varieties.)

How vainly men themselves amaze,
to win the Palm, the Oak, or Bays,
And their uncessant labours see
crowned from some single herb or tree....

ANDREW MARVELL, 17th century

Palm *(Phínikas)*

The palm tree was associated with Apollo, the god of light and music, who was born with his twin sister Artemis, goddess of the moon and the hunt, beneath its shade.This was described by Homer in his hymn to Apollo. The exotic palm tree was often used to decorate the area around sanctuaries. Pausanias, when visiting Boiotia in the 2nd century AD, recorded that a palm tree grew in front of a temple dedicated to Artemis. The leaf inspired ancient Greek art and the fan like palmette was a popular motif and frequently used in ornamentation. Wreaths of palm leaves were worn at banquets and crowns were used for winners of the games. The leaves were carried in triumphal processions and were symbolic of military victory.

Branches of palm were carried by the multitude when they went to greet Christ entering Jerusalem. The early church adopted the palm branch as a symbol of the Christian's victory over death.

This tall slender tree has grown since ancient times in Cephalonia. Today it is visible in gardens, decorating the streets in towns and occasionally standing proudly alone where once a villa had stood, lending an unexpected air of grandeur to the landscape.

Phoenix canariensis
Evergreen tree with fan-like leaves, flowers (February) and sprays of small dates (October-November). Grows up to a height of 20m.
(other species: *phoenix dactylifera*)

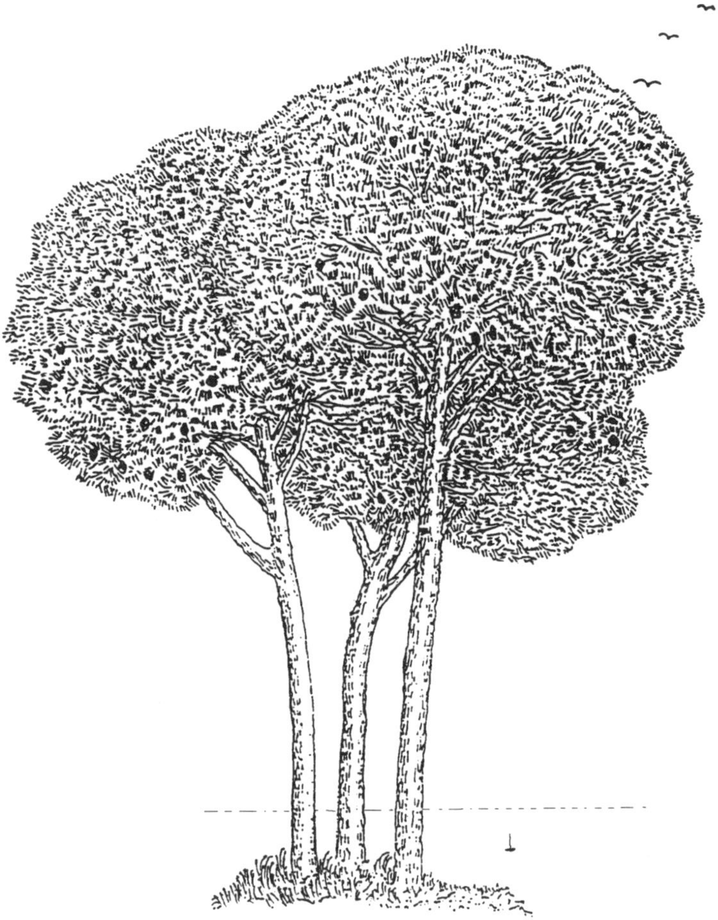

He fell; as falls an oak, or poplar tall,
Or lofty pine,which on the mountain top
For some proud ship the woodman's axe hath hewn.

Iliad 16.556. HOMER, 8th century BC

Pine *(Péfko)*

This tall dignified tree was named Pitys by the ancient Greeks. In mythology, Pitys was a wood nymph loved by Pan. She was also wooed by Boreas, the stormy north wind. However, Pitys favoured Pan because he was much more gentle and she loved his music. Consequently, in a jealous rage Boreas blew her over a cliff and the lifeless nymph was transformed into a pine tree by Gaia, the goddess of the earth. Even today, when the north wind blows, the transformed wood nymph cries for Pan, and teardrops of clear resin are sometimes to be seen on the tree.

The pine was also associated with Poseidon, the god of the sea. It was one of the best timbers to be used for ship building and the resin was used as pitch to seal boats. Pine resin was used as a preservative and also flavoured the wine. Today resin may still be tasted in the *retsína* wines of Greece. The ancient Greeks used pine kernels for a sweetmeat made with flour and spices.

The medicinal virtues of this tree were known to Hippocrates. Pine has always been regarded as healing for respiratory ailments. There are many pine woods in Cephalonia and their cool resin-scented air is restoring and refreshing.

Pinus pinea
Tall evergreen tree, umbrella-shaped when mature with reddish patches on the bark. Flowers (April-May). Large globular cones (August-September). Grows up to 30m.
Hill tops. (There are several species.)

As you go then along a mountain road by way of this rock, you reach a temple of Apollo surnamed Platanistius (god of the Plane tree grove).

PAUSANIAS, 2nd century AD

Plane Tree *(Plátanos)*

In ancient Greece this stately tree with its graceful spreading branches was considered to be a gift from the gods and was highly valued for its beauty and cool shade. Legend tells us that Hercules planted a celebrated grove at Olympia for his father Zeus. The plane trees which gave precious shade to the paths of Plato's academy were also famous.

Herodotus, the renowned Greek historian of the 5th century BC, wrote that Xerxes, King of the Persians, had so admired a magnificent plane tree in a valley in Lydia that he decorated it with golden ornaments and appointed a guardian for it in perpetuity. The well-known plane tree on the island of Kos under which Hippocrates was said to have taught his pupils still exists today.

A plane tree is an important landmark for the traveller, a place to rest from the unrelenting heat of the midday sun. Often a refreshing spring may be found nearby. This tree stands in many a village square in Cephalonia. At the monastery of St Gerasimos there are three fine plane trees that were planted by the saint in the 16th century.

Platanus orientalis
Deciduous tree with large deeply-cut leaves, clusters of flowers (April-May) and round bristly fruits (September-October). Grows up to 30m high.
Valleys, along streams and by the roadside.

Enclosed by a hedge, a great garden of lofty trees there were, bright and laden with pears, pomegranates, apples, very sweet figs and rich olives. In summer and winter alike, here with the breath of the west wind, fruit grows and ripens continuously. Pear upon pear matures to fullness, apple on apple, cluster on cluster of grapes, figs upon figs....There too, bordering the last two rows of vines, are trim plots of all kinds of herbs that keep fresh and fragrant all the year round. Lastly there are two springs of water, and one of these is channelled out over the whole space of the garden....

Odyssey 7.112. HOMER, 8th century BC

THE GIFT OF FRUIT

Then I will give you rain in due season,
and the land shall yield her increase,
and the trees of the field shall yield their fruit.
Leviticus, *26. 4*

Almond (*Amígdalo*)

The delicate blossoms of the almond tree are the first to appear after the winter. It is this tree that heralds the arrival of spring in Cephalonia.

Almonds can often be found for sale in the market and fine almond cakes are still made in the homes. A delicious almond cordial called *Soumáda* is made locally and may be purchased in cake shops. It is traditional for guests at weddings to be given this refreshing drink outside the church after the ceremony.

From texts that have survived from ancient Greece, we learn that it was the almond that was the most popular nut. Almonds were used, often combined with honey, for pastries, cakes and sweets. The oil was used for making ointments and valued in perfumery.

Amygdalus communis
Shrub or deciduous tree with narrow oblong leaves and pale pink to white flowers (January-February). Grows to a height of 7m. Stony land, rocky places outside villages, orchards and gardens. Fruit in season: August-September

Apple (*Mílo*)

According to legend, there was a garden at the world's end in the far west where a sacred apple tree grew. It was guarded by the Hesperides, "the daughters of the evening", who were helped by a serpent. They sang songs about the beautiful colours of the sunset and compared it with the colours of a fully-laden apple tree. As the setting sun disappeared below the horizon it appeared to them like a crimson apple sinking in to the western ocean. Soon afterwards Hesperus, the evening star sacred to Aphrodite, the goddess of love and beauty, rose up in the sky.

In mythology, the apple was sacred to Aphrodite and associated with love. The gift of an apple was a love token. In the 9th century, the Byzantine emperor Theophilus chose his bride by presenting her with a golden apple.

Malus communis
Deciduous tree with oval leaves and white flowers (April-May). Grows to a height of 6m. ✎ Gardens and orchards. Fruit in season: September-November
(There are several species.)

As a sweet apple at the tip of the uttermost bough,
forgotten by the gatherers of that plentiful tree.
No, not forgotten but quite out of reach,
O beautiful sweet apple high on the bough.
SAPPHO, 6th century BC

Apricot (*Verícoco*)

It appears that the apricot was introduced to Greece by 1st century AD and was first named "Armenian apple".

In Cephalonia, the sun dried stones are boiled in a syrup of cherries together with brandy to produce a delicious home-made liqueur.

Prunus armeniaca
Deciduous small tree with oval leaves and white or pale pink flowers (February). Grows to a height of 6m. Gardens and orchards. Fruit in season: May-June

Carob (*Haroúpi* or *Coútsoupo*)

The official name of this tree derives from the Greek word *cératon* meaning horn. It refers to its tough, dark brown pod. The seeds are uniform in size and were once used as the original carat weight of jewellers.

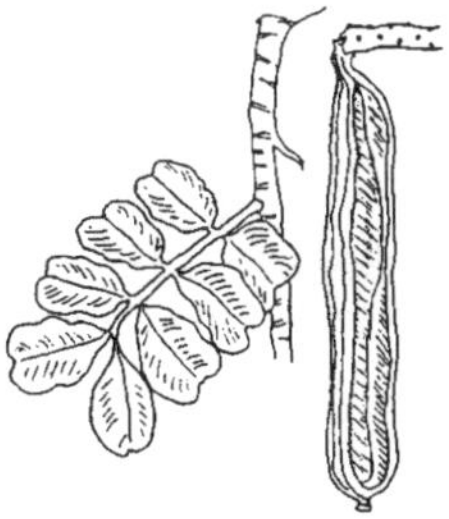

The ancient Greeks fed carob pods to their animals and in times of hardship they themselves also ate the pods. During the war in Cephalonia they used to make carob flour. Today in the villages people enjoy chewing the sweet nutritious pods and still feed them to domestic animals.

Ceratonia siliqua
Evergreen tree with leathery, deep green leaves. Tiny green or red flowers (October-November) and large brownish-purple pods. Grows to a height of 3-10m.
Dry rocky places, woodland and scrubland. Fruit in season: August-September.

Sour Cherry *(Vísino)*

In Cephalonia, they boil sour cherries together with sugar to make a tasty, popular "spoon sweet", *glikó koutalioú,* that is often kept in reserve for visitors. A spoonful of cherries glistening in a thick syrup is served on a dainty little glass dish, accompanied by a traditional Greek coffee and an icy-cold glass of water. "Spoon sweets" are also made from many other fruits (e.g. oranges, lemons, citrons, grapes, figs, quince and small aubergines). This delightful custom originated in Byzantium.

According to Theophrastus, it was the hard wood of the cherry that was utilised for making bows, spears and javelins. Pausanias recorded that the Trojan horse would have been constructed with cherry wood.

In Cephalonia, they boil sweet cherry stalks in water and use the liquid as a remedy for dissolving kidney stones.

Cerasus vulgaris
Small deciduous tree with oval leaves, small yellow flowers (February-March) and scarlet fruit. Grows to a height of 5m. Gardens and orchards. Fruit in season: July

Sweet Cherry *Cerasus dulcis*
Deciduous tree with oval leaves and pink flowers (February-March). Grows up to a height of 7m. Gardens and orchards. Fruit in season: June

Citrus fruits

Orange and lemon trees with their rich colourful harvest and dense evergreen foliage are a familiar sight all over Greece. However, it seems that they were not part of the landscape of ancient Greece. Citrus fruits are generally thought to be native to the Far East, and in ancient times they were cultivated in the Levant. The conquests of Alexander the Great in the 4th century BC brought lasting changes to Greek horticulture. He took trained observers with him on his expeditions through foreign eastern lands who recorded their discoveries. During the centuries that followed various cultivated plants and trees began to be brought from the East to the West. Of the citrus fruits, it appears the citron was the first to arrive, followed by the bitter orange and the lemon. The sweet orange reached Greece much later on.

In Cephalonia citrus trees are greatly appreciated and found in nearly every garden. The fruit can remain on the tree for months without becoming over-ripe, and it commonly occurs that the tree may bloom at the same time. The flowers of all these trees have a beautiful fragrance.

Orange
Citrus sinensis
(Portokáli)

Bitter orange
Citrus aurantium
(Nerági)

Lemon
Citrus limon
(Lemóni)

Mandarin
Citrus deliciosa
(Mandaríni)

Citron
Citrus medica
(Cítron)

Evergreen trees with dark green leaves and white flowers (mostly late winter and spring). All grow up to a height of 4-5m. Gardens and orchards. Bitter orange trees are found on roadsides and in squares. Fruit in season: November-June

Fig *(Sýco)*

In mythology, it was Demeter, the goddess of the harvest, who created the fig tree. Both fresh and dried figs were part of the staple diet of the ancient Greeks. Aristotle recorded that the milky juice of the fig was used as rennet in cheese-making. Since ancient times figs have been used for healing sores. The fig is split and applied hot. Its milky juice may also be used to destroy warts.

It is the fruit of the fig that is mentioned in the Bible more often than any other fruit. Together with the olive and the vine, it represented fortunate living and was a symbol of peace and plenty. In many areas of Cephalonia fig trees are found growing wild in the countryside.

Ficus carica
Deciduous, spreading tree with broad leaves and tiny flowers (January). Grows to a height of 7m. ✎ Grows wild on poor stony soil and in gardens. Fruit in season: June, August and September. (There are other varieties, one that produces figs in November)

For Isaiah had said, Let them take a lump of figs, and lay it for a plaister upon the boil, and he shall recover.
Isaiah, 38. 21

Loquat *(Moúsmoulo or Méspola)*

This attractive small tree with its sweet, bright yellow fruit originally came from China but has been growing in the Mediterranean region for the last few hundred years. In Cephalonia the loquat is the first tree of the year to produce fruit.

A spoon sweet is made with this fruit and it is served with almonds.

Eriobotrya japonica
Evergreen tree with large leathery leaves and clusters of white flowers (November). Grows to a height of about 10m. Found in gardens and in villages. Fruit in season: May-June

Mulberry (*Moúro*)

The ancient Greeks ate mulberries at their feasts. According to Dioscorides, the fruit was used medicinally for several ailments including digestive problems. Galen also mentions that the berries are beneficial to the health. Theophrastus recorded that, like the fig tree, its strong wood could bend easily and was useful for making certain objects.

The leaf of the white mulberry was used for feeding the silkworm. In the 6th century, the Byzantine emperor Justinian introduced the culture of silkworms to Constantinople and from there it spread to Italy and beyond.

In herbal medicine the dark purple liquid of the black mulberry was used widely as a syrup for sore throats, coughs and colds. Both the black and the white berries when fully ripe are regarded as a tonic and are excellent for the blood.

Black mulberry *Morus nigra* White mulberry *Morus alba*
Deciduous tree with oval or heart-shaped leaves and spikes of creamish-green flowers (April). Grows to a height of 20m. Roadsides and gardens.
Fruit in season: May-June

Our journey is to a feast, prepared by friends
For Demeter, now that she robes herself in harvest.
They have set aside the first-fruits as an offering
To thank her for a threshing-floor heaped with grain.
THEOCRITUS, 3rd century BC

Peach *(Rodákino)*

The peach seems to have been known in Greece by the 3rd century BC. At that time it was called the “Persian apple”.

A tea made from peach pits is cleansing and healing for wounds.

Prunus persica
Deciduous tree with oblong leaves and deep pink flowers (February-March). Grows to a height of 6m. Orchards and gardens. Fruit in season: June-July

Wild Pear *(Achládi)*

The wild pear was the first fruit known to have been eaten by humans in Greece. In ancient times it formed part of the poor man’s diet. Pear trees were also well known for their use as a defensive hedge.

Wild pears are still picked in the villages in Cephalonia today. They are often put into boxes and covered with straw to ripen and become sweet.

Pyrus pyraster
Deciduous tree with thin oval leaves and white flowers (March - April). Grows to a height of 5m. Dry stony land and hillsides. Fruit in season: October-November

The oldest image is made of wild pear wood.
PAUSANIAS, 2nd century AD

Persimmon *(Lotós)*

This pretty tree is grown in many gardens and in autumn, when it has almost lost all its leaves, it produces attractive orange fruit.

In Greece, this fruit is said to be the Lotos mentioned by Homer. Odysseus and his men on returning from the Trojan war visited the land of the Lotos-eaters. Some of his men ate the honey-sweet fruit and it had such an effect on them that all they desired was to stay there and feast on it for ever. They were happy to forget all thoughts of their homeland and had to be forced back to the ship in tears.

Diospyros kaki
Small deciduous tree with roundish leaves and yellowish-white flowers (April-May) and deep orange-coloured fruit. Grows to a height of 4m.
Orchards and gardens. Fruit in season: October-November

In the hollow Lotos-land to live and lie reclined
On the hills like gods together, careless of mankind.
For they lie beside their nectar, and the bolts are hurled
Far below them in the valleys, and the clouds are lightly curled ....
ALFRED, LORD TENNYSON, 19th century

Pomegranate *(Rógdi)*

In ancient Greece, the pomegranate was sacred to Hera, the goddess of marriage. It was also connected with the worship of Demeter, the goddess of the harvest. It symbolised life and fertility and was associated with Persephone, daughter of Demeter, who returned every spring to regenerate the earth.

This fruit is referred to many times in the Old Testament. The pomegranate motif was used in the decoration of King Solomon's temple and it was embroidered on the hem of Aaron's robe. In Christian times the pomegranate is symbolic of the Resurrection.

In the Orthodox Church it is traditional on the days when saints are commemorated to give *sperná* (a rich mixture of boiled wheat, pomegranate seeds, sugared almonds, raisins, nuts and spices flavoured with mint and parsley) to the congregation. *Sperná* symbolises the Resurrection and the Everlasting Life and follows an ancient custom.

Punica granatum
Deciduous shrub or small tree with oblong glossy leaves, large red flowers (May-June) and rosy-red fruit. Grows up to 5m.
Gardens. Fruit in season: October-November

"The statue of Hera is seated on a throne; it is huge,
made of gold and ivory and is the work of Polycleitus.
She is wearing a crown with Graces and Seasons
worked upon it and in one hand she carries a Pomegranate
and in the other a sceptre. About the Pomegranate I must say nothing,
for its story is somewhat of a holy mystery...."
PAUSANIAS, 2nd century AD

Prickly Pear Barbary Fig *(Barbarósyco)*

The wild spiny cactus was probably introduced by Crusader knights to the Mediterranean region. It produces sweet pink fruit with tiny spines. In war time it was a valuable fruit for the local population.

Opuntia ficus-indica
Cactus with bright yellow flowers (May-June) and pink fruit with prickles. Grows to a height of 4m.
Rocky hill slopes and roadsides. Fruit in season: August-September

Quince *(Cydóni)*

This ancient fruit tree was called "apple of Cydonia" after the place called Cydonia in Crete. In mythology, the quince was sacred to Aphrodite, the goddess of love and beauty, and was a symbol of love and marriage. In ancient times a newly wedded couple ate quince at their wedding feast. It was also a popular medicinal plant and it was used for digestive disorders, sore throats and coughs. Today it is still used for treating coughs and gastritis. The fruit of this variety of quince is sour and edible only when cooked. There is another variety which is sweet and smaller in size. In Cephalonia, an excellent preserve made with this fruit called *Cydonópasto* may be found in bakeries and cake shops.

Cydonia oblonga
Deciduous shrub or small tree with oblong leaves and whitish pink flowers (April). Grows to a height of 6m. Gardens. Fruit in season: November

Strawberry Tree *(Coúmaro)*

The sweet crimson fruit of the strawberry tree was served at the banquets of the ancient Greeks. In Cephalonia today the fruit is often made into jam. Strawberry tree fruit is mildly alcoholic and eaten in great amounts can be intoxicating. In some villages they make a liqueur from it.

According to Theophrastus, parts of looms were made from the wood of the strawberry tree. (see also p.109)

Arbutus unedo
Evergreen shrub or small tree with oval serrated leaves and whitish bell-shaped flowers (August-December) and crimson fruit with rough skin. The flowers and fruit often occur together. Grows to a height of 3-12m. Rocky hillsides and edges of woods. Fruit in season: November-December

Vine *(Staphíli)*

Since ancient times vines have been cultivated in Cephalonia. Vineyards are to be seen in many parts of the island. The famous *Robóla* white wine is produced from grapes growing in the areas of Valsamata, Troianata and Faraklata. This particular vine prefers the stony slopes of the higher ground. The road from the castle of St George to the monastery of St Gerasimos passes through one of the richest *Robóla* vine-growing areas. In Minies and Mavrata, on undulating land near the sea, they grow a different variety of vine called *Tsaoúsi.* A vine called *Zakinthinó* also grows in Mavrata. Fine dry white wines are produced from all these grapes. The celebrated sweet red wine *Mavrodáphne* mainly comes from vines growing in Lixouri and Thinia. *Muscatél* vines are also grown in various parts of the island. Cephalonia produces excellent quality raisins which were largely exported to England in the 18th and 19th centuries.

In ancient Greece wine had powerful religious associations. In mythology the vine was sacred to Dionysus, the god of wine. At banquets wine always accompanied a meal. Water was very often mixed with wine and sometimes honey and fragrant flowers were added. Wine was also believed to be a source of poetic inspiration and poets and sages for thousands of years have praised its pleasures and benefits.

Dioscorides mentioned that resinated wine was warming and a digestive. From modern research we learn that wine can even help to protect against heart disease.

A popular dish called *Dolmádes* is made with fresh vine leaves and rice. The vine is also valued for its shade. In summer, a well-trained vine can provide a bright green leafy roof for many a taverna.

Vitis vinifera
Woody climbing plant with deeply-lobed leaves, branched tendrils and greenish tiny flowers (April-May). Stony slopes, land outside villages and gardens.
Fruit in season : August-October

He went down to his father's spacious lofty-roofed store room
where heaped up lay gold and bronze, garments in chests and fragrant oil.
Along the wall in a line there were many large amphoras
full of old sweet wine without water, a divine drink for the time
when the wise Odysseus would return home after so many ordeals.
Odyssey 2.338. HOMER, 8th century BC

Walnut (*Carídi*)

The handsome walnut tree with its spreading boughs has been cultivated since ancient times. Walnuts were often served at banquets with the dessert. This tree was associated with Zeus. According to Greek legend the gods lived on walnuts.

In Cephalonia walnut trees were widely planted for their fruit and for their abundant shade. During the wars when the diet was poor, people ate the nutritious nuts and used to make tea from the dried leaves to keep healthy. In the villages today many people still drink walnut leaf tea. In herbal medicine the green outer casing of the nut and the leaves are mainly used for stomach disorders and as a digestive tonic.

They may also be used for skin problems. The green outer casing of the nut also yields a brown dye.

Juglans regia

Deciduous tree with large oval leaves. Grows to a height of about 20m.

Villages and gardens. Fruit in season: September-October

...and the fruit thereof shall be for meat, and the leaf thereof for medicine.

Ezekiel, 47. 12

View of St Efimia bay

Let us also marvel how the birds of the sky go out from their paradise:
they do not stay in one country but go, strong and weak alike,
over all countries at God's command, to all forests and fields.

PRINCE VLADIMIR MONOMAKH OF KIEV, 11th century

Downy oaks

Two men, two warriors in their prime....
So stood these two before the palace gates
As on the mountain side two towering oaks,
Which many a day have borne the wind and storm,
Firmly rifted by their strong continuous roots.

Iliad 12.144. HOMER, 8th century BC

APPENDIX

CELEBRATED ANCIENT GREEKS (referred to in the text)

HOMER 8th century BC

·HOMER·

In Homer's epics the *Iliad* and the *Odyssey,* plants are often mentioned. The *Iliad* tells us of events that occurred during a period of the Trojan war in Mycenaean times. The *Odyssey* tells us of Odysseus's journey home after the Trojan war to Ithaca (thought today by some people to be Cephalonia), the legendary temptations and perils that he faced during those twenty years of wandering, and the yearning he had for his homeland. Homer's poems are tales of domestic life and history together with legends and myths of a distant past. These ancient myths were the creation of men at a time when people had close associations with the natural world and the imagination was free and vividly alive.

HIPPOCRATES 4th century BC

HIPPOCRATES·

The physician who is traditionally known as the "Father of Medicine". He viewed the practice of medicine in a holistic way. He considered food, herbs, massage, medicinal waters, exercise, climate and occupation of great importance in regard to the treatment of illness. His medical ethics are still respected today.

ARISTOTLE 4th century BC

APISTOTELES

The renowned philosopher, scientist and biologist who studied in Athens under Plato. He was the founder of natural history and his works cover every branch of science and philosophy known in his day.

THEOPHRASTUS 3rd century BC

The Greek philosopher and botanist who is known as the "Father of Botany". He was a pupil of Aristotle and was greatly interested in natural history. He wrote two large botanical treatises and, as far as we know, Theophrastus was the first to attempt to classify trees as well as herbs and shrubs.

DIOSCORIDES 1st century AD

The physician and pharmacologist who visited many countries and industriously collected a vast store of information on plants. In his celebrated work *De Materia Medica* he includes about 500 plants. The original version did not survive but fortunately in the 6th century AD in Constantinople a copy was made for a Byzantine princess. It is illustrated with 479 paintings in colour on parchment and is a precious legacy of Byzantine scholarship. This magnificent treatise on herbal medicine remained a standard medical reference work in the West for over 1500 years and much of our present knowledge of medicinal herbs originates from Dioscorides.

ATHENAEUS 3rd century AD

The well known writer, whose only surviving work is called *Deipnosophistés*, "The Banquet of the Learned".

This important work is exceptionally interesting for its detailed descriptions of life in ancient times. It was written in the form of a series of dinner conversations between learned men all displaying their knowledge on various subjects including plants and botanical works.

GALEN 2nd century AD

The famous physician who treated the emperor Marcus Aurelius in Rome. He was also a doctor in the school for gladiators in Alexandria, and it was said that during Galen's term of office no gladiator died from wounds. He gathered together all the available medical knowledge of his day and divided plants into various medicinal categories which are known as *Galenic* to this day.

PAUSANIAS 2nd century AD

The celebrated traveller and writer. His books, taking the form of a tour of Greece, give accounts of cities, buildings and scenery, together with glimpses into daily life and descriptions of ceremonial rites and customs.

TRADITIONS

ST BASIL - 1st January

It is a custom on 31st December to go out into the countryside and dig up a sea squill (a bulbous plant similar to a very large onion with large green leaves). It is hung over the doorway of the house for good luck and health for the New Year. This tradition has survived from ancient times (see p.55). In Greece today sea squill is named after St Basil.

It is also a tradition for the New Year for someone to crack open a pomegranate by throwing it on the ground before the front door of the house. The released seeds signify the number of good things wished on the house and family (see p.93).

EPIPHANY - 6th January

On the eve of Epiphany the priest goes around his parish sanctifying every home with blessed Holy Water. For this he uses an *ayiastoúra* (a piece of wood decorated in the shape of a cone with rosemary and narcissi and often topped with a carnation).For Epiphany the church entrance is decorated with an arch consisting of myrtle (a classical symbol of everlasting love, peace and honour) and palm leaves (symbolising victory over death). If the parish is near the sea, a river or a lake, the water is blessed. The Holy Cross is thrown into the water, symbolic of the Baptism of Christ. Three pigeons are released, symbolic of the Holy Spirit.

THE ANNUNCIATION OF THE VIRGIN MARY - 25th March

For all the religious festivals people decorate special bread, *ártos,* with flowers and bring it to the church to be blessed. For the celebration of "The Annunciation of the Virgin Mary" the loaves are adorned with fragrant spring flowers, mainly sweet-scented freesias and stocks. On leaving the church each person is given a bunch to take home. The famous churches to visit for this memorable festival are in the villages of Faraklata, Pesada and Lakithra.

PALM SUNDAY

The church is decorated with palm leaves. Small crosses are made from palm leaves (symbolising triumph over death) and bound with branches of olive (symbolising peace), rosemary (symbolising remembrance), laurel (symbolising victory) and sage (symbolising salvation). These are called *váya* and each person in the congregation is given one by the priest.

HOLY FRIDAY

The *Epitáphion (*an oblong piece of stiffened cloth richly painted or embroidered in gold depicting the body of Christ laid out for burial) is placed on a wooden structure decorated with flowers. On the *Epitáphion* sweet scented leaves and petals are delicately scattered. It is a moving moment when the *Epitáphion* is carried in a candle-lit funeral procession around the parish to sanctify the area and the homes.

HOLY SATURDAY

In the morning, laurel leaves are scattered over the floor of the church, symbolising glory and victory over death. At midnight Easter is celebrated. It is a custom to take your candle home, trying not to let the flame go out on the way, bringing the "New Holy Easter Light" to the house for the rest of the year.

HOLY EASTER

The most important festival of the year is *Páscha,* Easter. It is celebrated with great rejoicing at a time of the year when magnificent wild spring flowers grace the hillsides and meadows and the countryside is bursting with new life.

After the long Lenten fast, lambs are barbecued and the famous red eggs that have been specially prepared for Easter days are eaten. Festive bread is baked for Easter called *lambrópsomo,* bread of the Bright Day. It was customary for the lady of the house to bake the bread on Holy Thursday. The bread is decorated with the sign of the Cross and a red egg in the centre. The red eggs are a Byzantine custom and symbolise the Resurrection of Christ. Red was the colour for royalty. The eggs should be dyed a deep rich red by boiling them together with a special sea weed which can be found in the Saturday market in Argostoli during the days leading up to Easter. It was traditional to decorate the eggs using delicate spring flowers and leaves and this charming custom is still followed by some people today.

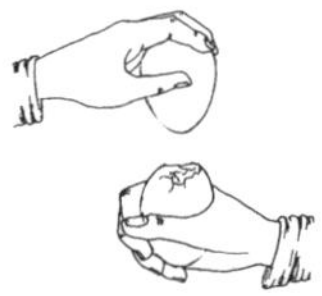

THE FIRST OF MAY

A wreath of colourful spring flowers and herbs can be seen hanging on nearly every front door, an ancient custom in celebration of spring. Traditionally, a bulb of garlic was included amongst the flowers because it was said to ward off all ills, misfortune and the evil eye.

ASCENSION DAY - Forty days after Easter

This is usually in May. It is traditional in the villages to scatter flowers and petals in the garden, in remembrance of family and friends who have departed from this life.

THE DORMITION OF THE VIRGIN MARY - 15th August

In all churches named after "The Dormition of the Virgin Mary" there are celebrations. In one particular church in the village of Pastra a miracle occurs each year. On 29th June (the day of the Twelve Apostles) Madonna lilies that bloomed during May are saved and placed beneath the icon of the Virgin Mary and left there until 15th August, by which time they are blooming again. From ancient times the Madonna lily has been a symbol of purity and since the first Christian times this graceful flower has been associated with theVirgin Mary.

ST GERASIMOS - 16th August

St Gerasimos, the patron saint of Cephalonia, lived in the 16th century. The people of the island together with pilgrims who have come from afar, celebrate the anniversary of his death at the monastery of St Gerasimos in the valley of Omala. It is a custom to follow the procession from the monastery down through a grand shady avenue to a place where one magnificent plane tree stands alone. It was on this site that St Gerasimos had built a well and personally planted a plane tree beside it. The procession stops here for a short while and it is traditional for people to take a leaf from the treasured tree in remembrance of their saint. On the 20th October, there is another similar celebration for St Gerasimos in remembrance of the day his body was found to be miraculously incorrupt.

Monastery of St Gerasimos

THE EXALTATION OF THE HOLY CROSS - 14th September

In all churches the Cross will be richly adorned with basil. In Greek, basil, *basilicós,* means "belonging to the king". This fragrant herb was found growing in the place where Saint Helen, mother of Constantine the Great, the first Christian emperor, reputedly found the true Cross of Christ in Palestine. After the service each member of the congregation is given a small bunch to take home. Basil is often seen growing in pots outside homes and is highly valued for its cool sweet aroma and bright little green leaves. Greeks take pleasure in offering a sprig as a sign of friendship. You may even notice a pot of basil beside the captain on the bridge of a ferry boat. Since ancient times this herb has been considered sacred and has never been used in traditional Greek cooking.

The custom of blessing the seeds of leguminous plants and cereals takes place on this day. Those who are going to sow seeds take a small selection wrapped in a handkerchief to the church. The seeds are left under the icon of Christ to be blessed. They are then taken home and mixed in with the rest.

THE ENTRY OF THE VIRGIN MARY INTO THE TEMPLE - 21st November

This feast is held during the middle of the sowing season. On this occasion the Virgin Mary is also called the Virgin Mary *Mesosporítissa* (Virgin Mary of the middle of the sowing season). In Her memory a traditional dish is made in the home out of many different local seeds – wheat, corn, beans, lentils, chickpeas, broadbeans and peas. This follows an ancient custom of offering seeds to Demeter, the goddess of agriculture, to ensure a good harvest for the next year.

CHRISTMAS - 25th December

The wild strawberry tree is full of cheerful, sweet red fruits at this time of year. It is customary to pick branches for decorating the home at Christmas. Branches of myrtle are also used.
Special bread is made for Christmas day called *Christópsomo*, the bread of Christ. It is decorated with the Cross around which are placed walnuts and almonds. In the old days when the people returned from the mid-night service, the father of the house would hold the bread over the fire pouring oil over it three times saying "Christ is born, the light grows". Each member of the family took a piece of bread to eat, the rest was taken to the stables to feed the animals in memory of the warmth the animals offerred Christ at his birth.

NEW YEAR'S EVE - 31st December

The people of Argostoli say 'goodbye' to the old year by walking in the main street of the town where the band plays and the choirs sing. They spray one another with fragrant perfumes.

....He causeth the grass to grow for the cattle, and herb for the service of man:
that he may bring forth food out of the earth; And wine that maketh glad the heart of man,
and oil to make his face shine, and bread which strengtheneth man's heart.
The trees of the Lord are full of sap; the cedars of Lebanon, which He hath planted;
Where the birds make their nests: as for the stork, the fir trees are her house.
The high hills are a refuge for the wild goats; and the rocks for the conies.
He appointed the moon for seasons: the sun knoweth his going down.
O Lord, how manifold are Thy works! In wisdom hast Thou made them all:
the earth is full of Thy riches....

Psalm 104.14

FESTIVALS OF CEPHALONIA

In Greece there are many festivals held throughout the year. The religious celebrations are called *Panigýria*. They begin on the eve of the festival day. They are very joyful occasions and often after the church service there are festivities held near by. Visitors are always very welcome.
Some of the important celebrations are listed below.

JANUARY 1st
St Basil, KERAMIES
A cake named after St Basil is shared at mid-night amongst the congregation of this church to celebrate the New Year.
The sharing of the New Year's cake is traditional in all homes.

JANUARY 6th

Epiphany, Sissiotissa Church ARGOSTOLI

After the morning service - the Bishop lowers the Holy Cross into the sea. There is a procession across Drapanon bridge. (see p.104)

FEBRUARY 10th

St Haralabos, LIXOURI

After the morning service - procession.

ONE MONTH BEFORE LENT

Carnival celebrations.

ONE DAY BEFORE CLEAN MONDAY

Carnival parade in the main square of Argostoli.

CLEAN MONDAY

First day of fasting for Lent - celebrations held in LASSI, LIVATHO, SKALA and LIXOURI. Flying kites, traditional food for fasting and dancing.

MARCH 25th

The Annunciation of the Virgin Mary, FARAKLATA

After the evening service on March 24th, traditional Cephalonian food and dancing. The Revolution of 1821 is celebrated and parades are held throughout Greece.

HOLY WEEK OF EASTER

HOLY TUESDAY

Sissiotissa Church, ARGOSTOLI

Towards the end of evening prayers - the famous 9th century Byzantine hymn "Kassiane's Anthem" is sung by the choir of Cephalonia.

HOLY THURSDAY

Service of the Passion held in all churches.

HOLY FRIDAY

Cathedral ARGOSTOLI

After the evening service, the Epitaphios is carried in a candlelit procession. (see p.105) The procession accompanied by the band of Cephalonia goes from the Cathedral down to the port, along the harbour, through the square and back to the Cathedral.

EASTER SATURDAY/SUNDAY

Church of the Archangels, ARGOSTOLI

Midnight service - procession with candles to the main square. Fireworks.

APRIL 23rd or FIRST DAY AFTER EASTER
St George DAVGATA
After the evening service - barbecue and dancing.

NEW MONDAY (after Easter)
St Paraskevi, FARAKLATA
Easter celebration After the morning service - picnic and dancing outside the church.

Prophet Elias, RAZATA (near the ancient walls at KRANI)
Easter celebration. After the morning service - picnic and dancing outside the church.

NEW TUESDAY
A celebration for the Virgin Mary
Monastery of Themata, AYIA EVFIMIA (High on the mountain above the village.) After the morning service - barbecue and dancing.

The Virgin Mary, KOUROUKLATA
After the evening service - barbecue and dancing.

NEW FRIDAY
The Life Receiving Fountain, St Andrews Monastery, PERATATA
After the morning service - procession and lunch at the monastery.

The Life Receiving Fountain, MONOPOLATA (Near Lixouri)
After the morning service - procession.

SUNDAY AFTER EASTER
St Thomas, Sissia Monastery near the village of SIMOTATA
After the morning service - procession to Church of The Annunciation, KASTRO (about 12 km) where the icon of the Virgin Mary remains for three weeks.

FOUR WEEKS AFTER EASTER
Sunday of the Samaritan Woman, Church of The Annunciation, KASTRO
After the service - procession back to the Sissia Monastery
Picnic and dancing on the land below the monastery.

Ascension Day (40 days after Easter), Church of the Ascension, SVORANATA after the evening service – barbecue and dancing.

Pentecost (50 days after Easter) Church of The Pentecost, TRAPEZAKI near MOUSSATA. After the evening service – barbecue and dancing near the church.

MAY 21st
St Constantine and St Helen, CARAVATHOS
After the evening service on May 20th - barbecue and dancing near the church.
St. Spyridon church, Argostoli.

JULY 2nd
The Placing of the robe of the Virgin Mary
The Virgin Mary "Diotissa" church, DIAS ISLAND.

JULY 11th
St Efimia, St Efimia village.
After the evening service on 10th July – barbecue and dancing.

JULY 17th
St Marina, VLACHATA
After the morning service - barbecue and singing.

JULY 20th
Prophet Elias, RAZATA (near the ancient walls and KRANI)
After the evening service on July 19th - barbecue and dancing.

Prophet Elias, FRANGATA (on the road from Argostoli to Sami)
After the evening service on July 19th - barbecue and dancing.

JULY 25th
St Anna, LAKITHRA
After the evening service on July 24th - barbecue and dancing.

JULY 26th
St Paraskevi, TROIANATA
After the evening service on July 25th - barbecue and dancing.

JULY 27th
St Panteleimon, POULATA (near SAMI)
After the evening service on July 26th - dancing and a dinner.

St Panteleimon, KONTOGOURATA
After the evening service on July 27th - barbecue and dancing.

AUGUST 6th
The Holy Transfiguration, Sotiros Church, KALIGATA
After the evening service on August 5th - picnic and singing.

The Holy Transfiguration, Sotiros Church, TRAVLIATA
After the evening service on August 5th - picnic and singing.

AUGUST 15th
The Dormition of The Virgin Mary, CHALIOTATA (near SAMI)
After the evening service on August 14th - barbecue and dancing.

The Dormition of The Virgin Mary, MARKOPOULO
After the evening service on August 14th - barbecue and dancing.

AUGUST 16th
St Gerasimos, St Gerasimos Monastery, OMALA
All night vigil on August 15th. After the morning service - procession. The choir of Cephalonia.

AUGUST 16th
Robola Wine Festival, VALSAMATA (at the area of the 40 wells)
In the evening - barbecue and dancing.

First week end after AUGUST 16th
Robola Wine Festival, FRANGATA
Evenings of Saturday and Sunday - barbecue and dancing.

AUGUST 23rd
The Dormition of the Virgin Mary, DEMOUTSANDATA
After the morning service - procession.
(local celebration held eight days after the official day)
The Dormition of the Virgin Mary, Monastery of Kechrionas, LIXOURI

SEPTEMBER 8th
Birth of the Virgin Mary, Erissos Monastery, Paliohersou, MESSOVOUNIA
After the evening service on September 7th - grill, dancing and singing.

Birth of the Virgin Mary, Atros Monastery, POROS
After the evening service on September 7th - barbecue and dancing.

Birth of the Virgin Mary, DILINATA
After the evening service on September 7th - grill, dancing and singing.

SEPTEMBER 14th
The Day of the Holy Cross, Estavromenos Monastery, PESADA
After the evening service on May 13th - barbecue and dancing.
Monastery of the Holy Cross, KIPOURIA near LIXOURI
After the evening service on September 13th - dancing outside the entrance to the monastery.

SEPTEMBER 24th
The Virgin Mary of Drapanon, ARGOSTOLI (church near the cemetery over the bridge) After the evening service on September 23rd - procession to St Spyridon church. ARGOSTOLI

SEPTEMBER 26th
St John The Evangelist, SARLATA
After the evening service on September 25th - barbecue and dancing.

OCTOBER 1st or 2nd
St Spyridon, ARGOSTOLI
After the evening service - the procession goes back to the Virgin Mary of Drapanon church near the cemetery.

OCTOBER 20th
St Gerasimos, St Gerasimos Monastery, OMALA
After the morning service - procession with the Band of Argostoli.

OCTOBER 28th
National Celebration of 1940, ARGOSTOLI
Parade in the main square.

NOVEMBER 30th
St Andrew, St Andrew's Monastery near PERATATA
After the morning service - procession.

DECEMBER 4th
St Barbara, PROKOPATA (in a cave under the bridge near the village)
After the evening service on December 3rd - *spernά* (see p.94) is given to the congregation.

DECEMBER 9th
St Anna, LAKITHRA
After the evening service on September 8th - barbecue and dancing.

DECEMBER 31st
Lithostroton (the main street), ARGOSTOLI
New Year carols and songs in the evening.
The band and the choir of Cephalonia.

Love all God's creation, the whole of it and every grain of sand.
Love every leaf, every ray of God's light! Love the animals, love the plants,
Love everything. If you love everything, you will perceive the divine mystery in things....
FYODOR MIKHAILOVICH DOSTOYEVSKY, 19th century